No One in I Land

No One in I Land

A Parable of Awakening

Patricia A. Pearce

Dedicated to all those
who are helping
change the dream.

I LAND

Once upon a No Time, People dwelled in The Realm where they all knew that even though they looked different from each other, they were actually all The Life that sometimes looked like Tree and sometimes like Water and sometimes like Raven and sometimes like Caterpillar and sometimes like Rock and sometimes like Bear and sometimes like Human.

In The Realm, People felt The Life breathing, laughing, playing, singing and dancing in them, and they delighted in how things were always coming into being and then disappearing

1

again, like a magical kaleidoscope. The Realm contained all moments and all beings that ever happened or ever could happen, so nothing was ever lost, and everything vibrated with beauty, joy and gratitude, inside a boundless, laughing Love.

Now People didn't call The Realm "The Realm," because it was everything anyone had ever known and there wasn't anything that wasn't The Realm, so you can see how it never occurred to them to give it a name.

But one day, many, many Realm dwellers somehow fell into a strange sleep that transported them into a strange, seemingly endless dream.

It wasn't the sort of nighttime dream you have when you're tucked in your bed all cozy and warm and visit all manner of magical places and meet all sorts of interesting people without your head ever leaving your pillow. In the strange sleep the people didn't need to be in bed at all to dream their dream. They dreamed their dream while they were doing all sorts of things, like walking the dog, or sorting the mail, or shoveling the snow, or brushing their teeth, or buying the groceries. That's why it was such a strange sleep, because although the people looked for all the world like they were awake, in fact they weren't.

In their dream, the people saw themselves in a strange way: each person was an I—separate and all alone—made by an I-in-the-Sky who was separate and far, far away. This made the people feel terribly lonely.

The place they dreamed was called I Land, and, having forgotten The Realm where nothing is ever lost, the people now thought that when they died they would disappear into a deep dark nothingness. This terrified them completely.

Now because they felt so afraid and alone, all the dreamers of I Land spent their days trying to convince themselves that they were more special than all the other I's in I Land. But no matter what they tried, on most days they could not shake the conviction that all the other I's in I Land were much, much better than they were. This left them feeling littler than little.

All this made I Land a very lonely and fearful place, though nobody ever really talked much about feeling lonesome or scared, because everyone could see that all of I Land's really special, important I's never felt that way.

THE EMPEROR

Then one day a Particular I, as he was fixing his evening cup of tea, noticed an unpleasant gnawing inside—like the dull stomachache he always got when he ate too much gingerbread. This vague ache told him he wasn't important enough and he simply *must* do something about it. Now this feeling wasn't new; in fact it visited him just about every day. But it always greatly troubled him since, with so many other I's all vying to be more important than the next, he didn't see how he could ever manage to distinguish himself.

This night, though, his discomfort was much worse than usual, so he sat down with his cup of tea and took some time to dwell on what a sorry person he was and indulge in a few miserly thoughts about other I's.

As he watched the steam rising from his cup, suddenly an idea came to him, and as he entertained it his stomachache began to fade and he smiled the biggest smile that I Land had ever seen.

The next morning, he called all the I Landers together so he could make a dramatic announcement. I-in-the-Sky had given him an astonishing revelation: he was destined to be the Emperor of I Land.

The people looked puzzled, so he tried to explain. As Emperor, he would be I Land's most important I of all, with the solemn responsibility to make all the important decisions. This weighty burden meant that he alone would need to have dominion over everything in I Land—the forests, the rivers, the animals, the land, the air, the oceans—even the people.

However, he assured the assembled I's, if they followed his wisdom and did as he said, they stood a good chance of becoming special too, though never quite as special as he.

When asked what made him so special, he gave a response he knew nobody could argue with: It's just the way I-in-the-Sky meant for things to be.

It stood to reason that I Land must have an I who was the most important I of all. And so, when he asked who was in favor of I-in-the-Sky's plan to proclaim him Emperor, the people looked at each other, shrugged their shoulders, and in a loud chorus all shouted, "I!"

That settled, the Emperor told them that from now on they could call him Your Royal I-ness.

EXPANDING THE IMPERIAL PORTFOLIO

For a time, once everybody had gotten used to having an Emperor and knew their place in the Imperial version of things, all went smoothly. But after a while the Emperor's stomachache returned, telling him he hadn't quite distinguished himself enough, and that what he really needed was to expand I Land's Imperial portfolio. He designated his favorite I's as elite Imperial Troupes, and gave them axes to chop down trees in the forest to make way for the growth of Imperial agriculture.

Soon the forest was filled with the frightful sounds of cracking branches and thudding trunks that sent the animals scurrying, wondering if this Imperial version of reality was such a good idea and hoping the humans would wake up soon from their strange sleep.

The Emperor's plan worked well; the Imperial silos soon filled to overflowing, and the Emperor grew richer by the minute. But he still had a gnawing feeling there might be more out there that he hadn't yet claimed as his own. So he deployed his Imperial Troupes with swords and shields to search out other lands, giving them very strict orders to seize anything and everything that could prove useful. If anyone gives you any trouble, he said, tell them you've been dispatched by the most very special I in all of I Land.

So the Imperial Troupes set out and found many faraway lands where they encountered strange WonderFull People with strange WonderFull Ways. Whenever they walked in the forest, the WonderFull People talked to Tree and sang with Bird, and sweetly asked Blackberry Bush for some berries. And at night the WonderFull People danced under the stars because they knew they had come from the stars and they knew that the stars were still inside of them.

The loyal Imperial Troupes took every far-off thing they could get their hands on, even some of the WonderFull People, since they knew the Emperor would need them to work his Imperial lands. They chopped down more of the forests, dammed up some of the rivers, and built big houses for themselves so they could live comfortably while they oversaw all of the Emperor's lands.

Over time the WonderFull People grew very sad. They stopped asking Blackberry Bush if they could please have some berries, and just began taking them instead. They stopped talking to Tree and singing with Bird. Eventually they even stopped dancing under the stars, because now they barely remembered where they'd come from and who they really were.

As the Imperial version of reality took hold, His Royal I-ness grew ever richer and more powerful. But in spite of it all, he suffered with a terrible secret: as the most important I in I Land, he was also the loneliest I of all. And sometimes at night he dreamed of running playfully through the forest like a child, splashing his feet in the clear happy brook and letting the fish nibble at his toes, foxes and deer running alongside him as they explored the forest together; and he dreamed of crystal rain falling, sparkling in the sun like little rainbow jewels, and he would laugh and laugh as the rain spattered his face and ran down his back.

He always felt very happy in these dreams and he would wake up chuckling and whistling. But in the blink of an I—in fact no longer than it took his personal attendant to fetch his robe and slippers—the reality of I Land returned, and the terrible loneliness settled upon him again, making him very, very sad. Some mornings, terrifying thoughts—unthinkable, horrible thoughts—came to him: he was going to die and when he died, he would no longer be a very special I. In fact, he may not be an I at all.

No One

One day, while all the people were busy living the dream, bearing their loneliness as they fought to be special, something very odd happened in one of the Emperor's small far-off lands.

In this wee land a tiny bit of a stirring quivered in the dream. Not so much that anyone really noticed, preoccupied as they were, but just enough for a Certain Someone to wake up from the strange sleep and find himself in The Realm (which is where everybody else was too, but being asleep, they couldn't know this).

Once awake, this Certain Someone could clearly see that all the people were dreaming and that I Land and the Imperial version of reality were just figments of their imagination. What was really real was The Realm and nothing more.

It struck him as quite silly that the people were working so hard to be important, and he burst into laughter. Why couldn't the people see that they were already everything? Why couldn't the people see that the stars still lived in everyone and everything? How could anyone be better than anyone else when they were all equally The Life?

Being awake in The Realm, this Certain Someone knew he was part of everything. He knew he was no more important than anyone else. He knew he was not a *one,* all alone. And so this Certain Someone decided henceforth to call himself No One.

No One wanted the people to wake from the strange sleep so they would also remember that they were in The Realm and be free of the terrible loneliness and fear of I Land. In hopes he could jog their memory, he began describing Realm realities. He told them they needn't worry about trying to be special because they were already completely splendid. They needn't worry about being rich because they already had everything they needed.

No One also told them that in The Realm there was no such thing as loneliness, because everyone was part of The Life. And best of all, No One said, there was no such thing as a deep dark nothingness that would swallow them up when they died, because The Realm contained everything and everyone that ever was and ever could be.

Though the dreamers of I Land had their doubts, they were intrigued, because it all sounded so promising and strangely familiar. Every now and then when they were around No One, something stirred in them that seemed to kindle hazy recollections of things long forgotten, and they found themselves feeling ever so much more alive. And sometimes when they looked into No One's eyes they saw something that for all the world looked like the shimmering light of a boundless, laughing Love.

The Emperor, however, was not intrigued. This was troubling news: if No One's very presence made people defect from the Imperial version of reality, and people really started believing that nobody was any more special than anybody else, it would have dire consequences for his Imperial authority.

And so the Emperor sent his Imperial Troupes to arrest No One. He wanted No One brought back to the Imperial palace so the Imperial authorities could charge him with a capital crime: violating paragraph 21.3 of the Imperial Code of Important Standing, which prohibits Imperial subjects from seeking to become a Most Highly Very Special I. The Emperor ordered the Imperial Troupes to execute No One, which they did in the meanest of ways.

THE ONE

For the Emperor, this was a happy end to an unsettling story. For the people, it was something else altogether.

No One, it turned out, was not so easy to annihilate.

The trouble began when people began noticing mysterious occurrences—a ghost-like figure resembling No One strolling down a city street, a shimmering light that appeared in the bread when people broke it at suppertime, the soft sound of No One's laughing voice whistling in the wind around the door. Even more astonishing was that quite a few people started feeling a boundless, laughing Love inside that made them so giddy, all they could do was dance down the street, offering their luminous bread to anyone who happened along.

These odd occurrences convinced people that something very peculiar was going on. Maybe No One hadn't disappeared into the deep dark nothingness, after all?

The only way they could explain it was that No One must have been the Most Special I that had ever lived in I Land, so everyone started calling him *The One*.

Well, as you can imagine, this greatly upset the Emperor, as it was unmistakable evidence the people were beginning to forget that *he* was the most important I in I Land. The existence of a One who wasn't him was simply unbearable.

And so the Emperor called an emergency meeting of the Imperial Think Tank to help him decide what to do.

The Imperial Thinkers concluded the problem could easily be solved simply by killing some of The One's street dancers and bread sharers. But when the Emperor followed the Thinkers' advice, he soon found it only made matters worse. According to Imperial Intelligence, The

One's followers were completely unafraid of the deep dark nothingness. This created a very grave situation for His Royal I-ness.

Just when things seemed to be getting out of hand because the street dancers and bread sharers were multiplying and making more and more people unafraid, the most shocking thing of all happened. The Emperor himself announced he had become a believer in The One.

It was a magnificent turn of events that even the Think Tank Thinkers couldn't have thought up: now the Emperor could tell all his Imperial subjects that The One would make him into the most splendiferous, mighty Emperor ever.

But first His Royal I-ness needed everyone to agree on details concerning The One: who he was and why I-in-the-Sky had sent him to I Land. The Emperor called a special council to settle these important matters and, once an agreement had been reached, the Official Truth was engraved on a gilded plaque and unveiled, with much fanfare, as the new Holy Imperial I-Con.

Some of The One's Special Representatives were given Exclusive Rites to be sharers of the shimmering bread and they got to wear fancy robes and hats—much like the Emperor's—and from then on, whenever the Emperor dispatched the Imperial Troupes to far-off lands, some of The One's Special Representatives went along to explain who The One was. Henceforth, they explained, everyone would have to obey the Emperor without question, because he was, after all, the one The One had chosen to be I Land's most important I of all.

THE EMPEROR'S
I-DEALS

The people continued dreaming their dream and the Emperor grew richer and more powerful than ever. But after a while, sending the Imperial Troupes to far-off lands became just too difficult and expensive, and the Emperor wanted more efficient ways to make the far-off people his Imperial subjects. So the Think Tank came up with a plan.

Instead of sending the Imperial Troupes out with swords and shields, they sent the Emperor's

Men out with neckties and contracts to visit the little kings in far-off lands and present them Offers They Couldn't Refuse. The Emperor's Men offered to help some little kings build fancy I-Ways in exchange for the fruit that grew in their Magical Forests. Other little kings were promised good jobs for their subjects if they let the Emperor build sparkling I-Doll factories in their lands; one little king even agreed to let the Emperor's bulldozers dig the gleaming gold out of the Magical Mountains in a place the Emperor called his Mine.

Not long after most of the little kings had signed on to the Emperor's irresistible I-Deals, new obstacles sprung up. The Magical Forests didn't produce enough fruit to satisfy the Emperor, so the kings started cutting down the magical trees to sell to the sparkling factories where they could be made into I-Dolls. And the Emperor's Mine began to spew so much malodorous, gooey stuff into the rivers that the people had to go around holding their noses, which made it hard for them to operate the bulldozers to dig the gleaming gold. And the people working in the sparkling factories had to toil longer and longer days to pay for their tiny shacks and their daily bread.

The people began feeling disgruntled with the arrangement, but the Emperor's I-Deals came with No Money Back Guarantees, so they were stuck.

The Emperor, meanwhile, was feeling very proud of his brilliant strategy, because now he controlled almost all the far-off lands, and his Imperial warehouses were brimming with magical I-Dolls and gleaming gold.

THE EMPEROR'S NEW FOES

One glorious day, as the Emperor was strolling in his Imperial gardens feeling particularly pleased with himself, out of the corner of his eye he sensed someone shadowing him. This shocking apparition wasn't someone clamoring to take his picture or get his autograph—he was perfectly accustomed to that—but someone who never said a word and never showed his face. Most disturbing, this shadowy figure began mimicking everything he did. When the Emperor stomped his feet and shook his fists to try scaring him away, his shadowy follower mirrored him back. This made the Emperor very mad, and very determined.

So His Royal I-ness convened the Imperial Think Tank and the most important I's of the Imperial Troupes to assess this new threat. But before taking serious action, they decided they needed to name the Emperor's sinister stalker. The Think Tankers wanted to call him Nefarious Evil. They thought it sounded sophisticated, but the others thought it sounded silly—why use a word that everybody would have to look up in the dictionary? The Troupers wanted to call him Malevolent Evil because it sounded much scarier. The discussion went round and round, until finally the Emperor broke the impasse: the stalker would henceforth be known as the Nefarious Malevolent Evil (or NME, for short). The Imperial Authorities immediately called a press conference to inform the Imperial Times about the troubling developments. The next morning the headlines trumpeted the news of the Nefarious Malevolent Evil threatening all of I Land.

Because the situation was so dire, the Authorities assembled the Imperial Emporium and told them that there was only one alternative: to declare war. The Imperial Emporium agreed, and since the NME clearly intended to destroy all of I Land, the Emperor christened his campaign the War on Destruction. The Imperial Troupes unveiled their special Freedom Fireballs (which they'd always hoped to use one day), and the Emperor ordered all the armament factories in I Land to build the biggest, most powerful anti-destruction fireballs imaginable.

The Emperor told his Imperial subjects they were embarking on a heroic struggle, and as I Land's most important I, he humbly accepted his difficult destiny: to rid I Land of the Nefarious Malevolent Evil.

Many people were skeptical, but His Royal I-ness was the Emperor so he must know things they didn't. And of course since I-in-the-Sky was on their side—not to mention that they did have the best fireballs around—everything ought to work out. So why worry?

THE EMPEROR'S NEW WOES

Time passed and the War on Destruction dragged on and on without a single decisive victory. No matter how many fireballs they made and no matter how many Troupes they dispatched, the Imperial Authorities were unable to conquer the NME. In fact, it seemed the more they displayed Imperial force, the bigger and stronger the NME became.

But that wasn't all. Now that so many of the Magical Forests had been cut down to produce I-Dolls, the people started noticing a strange

29

stickiness in the air. The stickiness coated every-thing and was nearly impossible to wash off. Even simple things like eating soup became agonizingly burdensome—people's spoons stuck to their hands and mouths, and extrication was excruciating.

As life grew increasingly difficult, people began feeling a renewed appreciation for the Magical Forests, and they looked forlornly at their I-Dolls, wishing they could be made back into trees.

The situation had grown serious, so the Emperor convened his Think Tank to consider what to do. Since their fireballs were so advanced, the Thinkers reasoned, they could surely clear up the sticky air. So, just as I Land began having so many bad air days that nobody wanted to leave home, the Emperor announced the launching of Operation Air Freedom. Imperial aeroplanes streaked across the sky, detonating fireballs high up in the atmosphere. It was a breathtaking sight, witnessing the glory of Imperial ingenuity—as thrilling as watching the fireworks on I Land Day!

But rather than solving the problem, the fireballs made the stickiness even worse. This greatly troubled the Emperor and his Think Tank—never before had they encountered a problem that fireballs could not solve. They thought perhaps if only they made them bigger or smaller or aimed them more carefully, the fireballs could be made to work. So they set all the Imperial Scientists and Engineers to the task.

As though the War and the sticky air weren't enough, one day, when the Head of Imperial Investments surveyed the Imperial storehouses to inventory the Emperor's I-Dolls, he discovered, to his great dismay, that they had all melted into puddles of grey goo. Though he speculated that the goo may have been the result of having too many I-Dolls all in one space, the Imperial Investigators investigated and the Imperial Interpreters interpreted and for the life of them they couldn't be sure what had happened, or how to keep it from happening again.

In no time, the I-Doll goo epidemic spread all across the land, leaving grey puddles oozing out around every bank in I Land. It was a frightful situation because all the Emperor's Bankers and all the Emperor's Men couldn't get the I-Dolls to solidify again.

When Imperial Intelligence instructed all the I Landers to stockpile ample quantities of goo glue to guard against the epidemic, the people began wondering if the Emperor really knew what he was doing. But this wondering frankly caused them great consternation, because if His Royal I-ness couldn't get everything under control, then which I could?

Things were getting quite gloomy in I Land, and the people began to despair that the deep dark end would soon be upon them.

Wonder Full Ways

About this time, an even bigger threat to I Land was developing below the Imperial radar, something more troublesome than the War on Destruction, or the I-Dolls' grey goo, and something the Imperial apparatus was completely powerless to stop.

Certain I's began to suspect something fishy about the Imperial version of reality when they began noticing things this "reality" just couldn't account for, and soon they began stirring in the strange sleep. While having breakfast, some noticed that their orange juice gleamed with Life and they could hear the faint sound of a laughing Love in the popping bubbles of the froth. Others would just be going about their daily tasks when all sorts of perplexingly helpful accidents began occurring that left them wondering if their small lives were connected to something much bigger. Others, while walking in the woods wondering why I-in-the-Sky had to be so far, far away, were startled to see a We-in-the-Trees. Suddenly and shockingly, it occurred to them that they may not be separate and alone.

Could it be that they'd been dreaming their whole life long? Could it be that I Land was a make-believe story? When these astonishing experiences first began rousing many I's from the strange sleep, some were left quite shaken, and many went to see their I Doctors, in hopes of regaining their I sight.

In time, certain I's fully emerged from the dream and woke entirely into The Realm, realizing they had always been splendid and had never been alone. And because they could see that none of them was any more special or any less important than anyone else, they all started calling themselves No One.

Although the No Ones could now see that they were all expressions of The Life, just like all the other beings, I Land had kept them asleep for so long that they'd forgotten how to talk with Tree, Bear, Water, Raven, Rock and Caterpillar. So the first thing they did was set out in search of the last of the WonderFull People who still lived deep in the remaining Magical Forests, keeping alive the knowledge of the WonderFull Ways.

When the No Ones found the WonderFull People and told them their story of awakening from their dream, the WonderFull People danced and sang. Soon the WonderFull People began teaching the No Ones how to listen to Raven, not just with their ears, but with their hearts, and how to feel Tree's roots in their own feet and how to feel their own skin in Tree's bark, and how to bow to Blackberry Bush, how to sweetly request some of her luscious berries and how to give her thanks.

It took a while, but eventually the No Ones relearned these ways, and when they did, they set out for the Magical Mountains where they told their story to Tree and Raven, Water, Rock and Caterpillar. They told them about how they had dreamed a place called I Land where everything was separate and alone. And Tree and Raven, Rock and Water, Caterpillar and People laughed and laughed and laughed at such a funny idea.

But after a while the No Ones had a troubling realization: Bear was nowhere to be found. They asked where she was because they needed to tell her their story, too. Tree drooped her branches and Raven looked very sorrowful and said that Bear was not well.

Raven took them to the cave where Bear lay, barely breathing. Raven explained that the stickiness had been especially hard on Bear. Whenever it rained, Bear's sticky fur would get matted down and when it dried it turned hard, just like a shell, which made it almost impossible for Bear to even breathe.

That's when the No One People first began realizing that their dream had caused great harm. With heavy hearts, they gathered around Bear to tell her their story. They told her all about I Land, and when they were done Bear laughed a weak, wheezing laugh and whispered her congratulations to them for waking up from their I-bernation. But tears were running down her face, and down the people's faces too.

As the No Ones continued exploring the Magical Mountains, they were dismayed to discover that many of their friends were gone, and that where there used to be dancing trees now there were only lifeless stumps.

Regretting more and more their long slumber, the No Ones quickly set about doing whatever they could to tend and mend all that had been harmed by their dream of I Land. And they promised the WonderFull People they would help them protect the remaining Magical Forests from the Emperor's Men who were still trying to convince everyone that what they really needed, more than trees and rivers, were the Emperor's I-Dolls.

No One
Returns
to I Land

After a while, the WonderFull People urged the No Ones to go back and help everyone awaken. When the No One People returned to their I Land cities and towns, it was clear that everyone was still in their dream, believing themselves to be utterly separate, still struggling to be special, still filled with terror of the NME and of the deep dark nothingness.

All of this now seemed very funny to the No Ones, because they could clearly see that everything and everyone was equally The Life; they could see that the NME was simply the Emperor's shadow, that the deep dark nothingness was just an idea, and that nobody was ever lost or alone. But the No Ones also felt compassion for the people, because they still remembered how lonely and frightening it was to live in I Land.

Now, the No Ones understood that there are many ways to wake from a dream. If the dream is scary, you wake with a start in a most disagreeable way. If it's a pleasant dream, it simply fades away with the rising sun. And sometimes, best of all, a dream is so very funny that the dreamer wakes from it laughing out loud.

The No One People could see that the dreamers of I Land were headed for a very harsh awakening, and they were suddenly overcome with an uncontrollable urge to play with the dream. So they began doing unusual, bewildering things.

The No One gardeners snuck out one night and planted flowers so thick along all I Land's I-Ways that the next day the Emperor arrived at all of his important engagements with lily pollen blanketing his clothes and clogging his nose. The

No One janitors who worked at Imperial Head-quarters hid jack-in-the-boxes in all of the briefcases; when the Emperor's Men with their neckties and contracts tried to present Offers They Couldn't Refuse to one of the little kings, the jacks would jump up in their faces and make them laugh out loud to see just how silly the Emperor's offers were. The No One mechanics smeared chocolate inside the exhaust pipes of all the I-Mobiles, so that pretty soon every street smelled like a candy store. Whenever they poured a city sidewalk, the No One concrete workers drew hopscotch lines in the wet cement, and during the morning hustle-bustle of everyone rushing to work, the No One secretaries and executives in their sophisticated suits stopped right then and there to play a game of hopscotch, which made everybody else slow down just long enough to smile.

The No One musicians gathered in subway stations and on street corners, singing and playing the music of The Realm, warming the hearts of all the weary I's headed home from work. And the No One artists painted enormous paintings of flowers and feathers and animals, and when they unfurled their stunning images from the tops of the tallest buildings in I Land, the people gasped, then laughed and even danced, because never before had they noticed the Beauty.

All of this frolicking made things very hard for the Emperor of course, since he depended so much on people taking I Land very seriously. He and Imperial Intelligence set up jack-in-the-box checkpoints, banned paint-brushes, installed hopscotch surveillance cameras, and decreed that chocolate, lilies, and music in public places violated the Imperial Code of I Land Security.

But the more the Imperial Authorities tried to halt the playfulness and creative splendor, the more quickly it seemed to spread.

Meanwhile, as if everything were perfectly normal, the No Ones kept going to work and cleaning their houses and paying their bills. They bought season tickets to the I-Ball games (though now they cheered for *all* of the players), and they sat in coffee shops reading I Landish stories in the Imperial Times. But every now and then, a No One walking down the street would notice someone whose eyes twinkled with laughing Life, and they would wink at each other as they passed. And if they happened to meet on the bus or at a party, they wouldn't ask the usual I Land questions like "What's your name?" or "Where are you from?"

because they already knew the answers: they were No One and they came from the stars.

Instead, a No One would lean over and whisper, "What part are you playing?" And the other would whisper back something like, "A receptionist at the I Strain Clinic" or "A cameraman for I Witness News." And they would flash each other a knowing smile.

By now, because of the unrelenting War on Destruction and the sticky air and the I-Doll goo, many of the dreamers asleep in I Land were increasingly upset with the Emperor and his entire Imperial apparatus. But the No Ones knew they too were just playing their part in the dream.

Gradually, more and more people started waking up from the strange sleep, and soon they found themselves in The Realm, knowing they were all No One. How this was happening was something of a mystery. More seasoned No Ones attributed it to paroxysms of giggling that erupted whenever the Emperor summoned his Imperial subjects to the Imperial Square for an official announcement about the latest strategy to defeat the NME, or the most recent I-Doll solidification program. The giggling fits were virulently con-tagious—a tittering would ripple through the crowd, eventually erupting into massive raucous laughter, which always made the Emperor's face turn very red, and he would stomp indignantly back into his palace.

Others speculated that the awakenings came about simply because some people had slept long enough. They might be doing something quite ordinary like shuffling out to the driveway in their bathrobe and slippers to pick up their copy of the Imperial Times, and they would feel a tingling in their feet that spread through their whole body and soon they would notice something quite weird: the terrible loneliness began to lift. This made them so gleeful that they hurled the Imperial Times high up in the air, sang at the top of their lungs to the chirping birds, or kicked off their slippers to play hide and seek with the scampering squirrels.

Or maybe the real reason the people were waking up was that whenever the moon was full, clusters of No Ones would gather around a bonfire with the birds and the animals, and imagine all the people waking from the dream. In the flickering light of the fire and the silver glow of the moon, they would weave stories of the Magical Forests alive and thriving once again and of the People dancing and singing once more under the stars. And as they told their fireside stories, the No Ones themselves would chant and sway, then dance with all their might until they felt the stories come alive inside their very bones. And when the dancing and singing had finished and silence returned, they would feel an electric swirling in the wind and they knew that something had forever changed.

However this transformation was unfolding, the number of No Ones grew and grew. And soon, the Magical Forests began to thrive again. And whenever the Authorities came along and displayed the Imperial edicts ordering people to join the Imperial Troupes for the War on Destruction, the No Ones laughed and laughed and laughed, and sometimes in their laughing they would slap the Imperial Authorities on the back. And every now and then, this simple gesture was all it took to make some of the Imperial Authorities wake from the dream. And when they looked at the document in their hands and read it, they too laughed and laughed and laughed.

THE EMPEROR'S NEW LOWS

One day, after all the others had awakened from their strange dream, the Emperor was pacing about his Imperial Gardens pondering his latest plan for a new fireball massive enough to annihilate the NME and the sticky air in one gargantuan fiery blast. As he puzzled over one last detail—how to keep the rest of I Land from being incinerated—something startled him out of the corner of his eye. Whirling around, fists raised, the Emperor braced himself to come face to face, at last, with the NME. But all he saw was his own shadow taunting him from the green grass beneath his feet.

Suddenly an immense weariness overcame him, sucking the last bit of willpower from his bones, and he collapsed like a marionette cut from its strings. Lying immobilized in the puddle of his shadow, the Emperor was filled with horror: he would never be able to defeat the Nefarious Malevolent Evil, or explode the sticky air, or save the I-Dolls from their grey goo. His stomachache returned with a vengeance, telling him he was the sorriest Emperor I Land had ever seen.

Wishing the deep dark nothingness would just take him, the Emperor sobbed, and sobbed. He cried so hard and so long that little rivulets of tears coursed across the lawn and trickled over the edge of the Imperial reflecting pool. He sobbed and sobbed until there were no more tears left.

Clean empty, he opened his eyes and saw something that startled the bejesus out of him. Standing not an arm's length away was a deer looking him straight in the eye.

Still as a statue, the deer beheld the Emperor with eyes that were dark pools of gentleness. The animal's delicate, disarming gaze touched some long-forgotten place deep inside the Emperor, awakening in him the strange realization that he and the deer were one.

When the Emperor blinked in disbelief, the spell was broken and the deer bounded off over the rose bushes. Then, as the Emperor began looking around, he noticed things that simply amazed him. The droplets of tears still clinging to the grass were sparkling like little rainbow jewels, and he could swear the breeze rustling through the trees was speaking to him—to *him!*—and the birds perched in the tree branches were singing a melodious sonnet that echoed a long-forgotten song in his own heart.

This was a Realm he never knew existed, where there was no such thing as an NME or a gooey I-Doll. Like a flash of lightning, the Emperor had an I shattering realization: everything was *everything!*

Now knowing for a fact that he wasn't alone, and giddy with happiness, he leapt to his feet and right then and there danced a jig.

Suddenly he froze mid-jig, and his jaw dropped at the magnitude of a new, even more astonishing revelation: he could see something the other I Landers couldn't, which could only mean one thing: he *was* special. So special, in fact, that he might well be The One that I-in-the-Sky had sent to save I Land.

Now, he realized, he had been given a Very Important Task: to open all the other I's of I Land.

Right away he ordered the Imperial trumpeters to trumpet from the palace parapets to summon his subjects for a very dramatic announcement, and when all the No Ones had gathered in the Imperial Square he told them he had very important news to tell them, that *everything was everything!*

The No Ones, delighted that the Emperor had awakened, let out a loud whoop and began laughing a raucous laughter.

Sure they were making fun of him, the Emperor stormed back into his palace, incredulous that they would dare to ridicule such a special message. This Very Important Task, it seemed, was going to be more difficult than he had realized.

If his subjects wouldn't listen to him directly, he would have to find another way to get his message across. So he ordered the Imperial aeroplanes to fly above the Imperial Square every hour on the hour, skywriting: "EVERYTHING IS EVERYTHING!"

Every hour on the hour the No Ones would watch the aeroplanes flying overhead, dumbfounded that the Emperor was still going to so much effort to state the obvious, and concerned that maybe his awakening hadn't really taken hold.

The Emperor, meanwhile, looking out from his palace window, saw the stunned expression on people's faces, and realized they *still* didn't understand.

The Emperor's Very Important Task was beginning to weigh on him like a huge sack of potatoes flung across his shoulders; he worried that if he failed to find a way to open all the I's of I Land his stomachache would return and never go away.

Glumly pacing the Imperial gardens once more, the Emperor considered what else he could try. He paced and agonized, agonized and paced until his feet were blistered and his brow furrowed and drenched with sweat. Just as he was about to give up, an idea flashed into his mind, one that was guaranteed to awaken the I Landers from their stupor.

Not wasting a moment, the Emperor dispatched an order: the Imperial Engineers would set out to design the biggest alarm clock I Land had ever seen and would install it in the middle of the Imperial Square.

Every hour on the hour the gargantuan alarm clock rang with such a clamoring ring that all the No Ones had to cover their ears from the deafening cacophony.

Watching from his window, the Emperor was dismayed to see that not only were the I Landers still looking dumbfounded at the sky-writing proclamation, but now they were covering their ears so they wouldn't hear the alarm clock. What a stubborn people his subjects were!

Going back to the Imperial gardens to pace yet again, the Emperor began to wonder if he'd been going about this all wrong. Maybe now that he'd had his special I Opening he also had special powers and could awaken the I Landers with the Force of his Will.

So he scrunched up his face and thought and thought, imagining all of his subjects' faces lighting up with the realization that everything was everything, and glowing with adoration for him, as he was The One who brought them this spectacular revelation.

But no matter how hard he thought, every day the I Landers continued looking dumbfounded and covering their ears.

By now the Emperor was despondent. Not only was he out of ideas, but even worse he could no longer see the sparkling rainbow jewels in the drops of dew, or hear the melodious song of the birds in his heart. The Realm had completely vanished from his sight, leaving him with only an empty longing.

If only he'd had a wise old sage who could tell him what to do. But alas, all he had was the Think Tank.

With nothing else to try and nothing more to lose, the Emperor summoned the Thinkers to see if perchance they could propose ways he could fulfill his Very Important Task.

The Emperor began by recounting the story of his encounter in the gardens with the deer, and how he knew then that everything was everything.

Seeing that the Thinkers' eyes were twinkling with a joy he had never before noticed, the Emperor grew hopeful that perhaps at last his message was getting across. Then he confided why he had gathered them: now that he knew he was The One I Land had been waiting for he needed their help in carrying out his Very Important Task of opening all the I's of I Land.

The Think Tankers began to stifle giggles. They tried very hard to restrain themselves. They bit their lips and hugged their sides, but it was no use. Soon their titters erupted into loud guffaws which exploded into raucous laughter. They laughed and laughed, and in their laughter one of them slapped the Emperor on the back.

He blinked.

Then, remembering what he had just been dreaming—that he was Emperor in a place called I Land, where everyone was separate and all alone— the new No One laughed and laughed until his stomach ached.

The Wondrous Realm

An electric swirling in the wind told all the No One People what had finally happened. Flocking to the Imperial Square to welcome the last No One into The Realm, they sang the song they'd eagerly been waiting to sing: "The Emperor has no foes! The Emperor has no woes!"

Relieved to know he was indeed No One, grateful he didn't have to be special anymore, the former Emperor was overcome with joy. His burdensome stomachache, the terrible loneliness and the fear of the deep dark nothingness—all had vanished. He knew now that he had been splendid all along and that he had never really left The Realm which had visited him from time to time in divine dreams of running with the foxes and deer through the forest.

Once again all the People could feel The Life breathing, laughing, playing, singing and dancing in them. And when nighttime came they would join the birds and the trees and all the animals—dancing and singing together under the stars—because now everyone and everybody together remembered they had come from the stars and that the stars were still inside them.

And sometimes, when the stars were especially bright and the breeze was blowing just so, People would look all around and begin to cry. At first Tree and Raven and the other birds and animals thought this odd. But after a while, they got used to it. People cried not because they were sad, but because they understood the gift their lonely dream had given them.

Now that the People knew what it was to be an I, they could see just how amazingly beautiful it was to be part of this wondrous Realm, where nothing was ever lost and nobody was ever alone. And with tears still glistening on their cheeks they danced faster and sang louder than ever before, because finally they could see what an astounding miracle it is to be this boundless laughing Love.

About the Author

Patricia Pearce is a writer, speaker, and spiritual teacher. A former pastor, she lives in Philadelphia, Pennsylvania. Learn more about her work and download a free study guide for *No One in I Land* on her website.

www.patriciapearce.com.

ALSO BY PATRICIA PEARCE

Beyond Jesus: My Spiritual Odyssey

8,000 WORDS MAY

Printed in Great Britain
by Amazon

31397563R00038